Under
New
Management

Under
New
Management

SAMUEL GORDON

AMBASSADOR PRODUCTIONS LTD.
16 HILLVIEW AVENUE
BELFAST BT5 6JR

455 GREAT WESTERN ROAD
GLASGOW G12 8HH

Printed in Great Britain by Ambassador Productions Ltd.

CONTENTS

1. A Change of Address   9

2. God's Love Gift   12

3. Under New Management   15

4. Heaven's Royal Crest   18

5. Engaged to be Married   21

6. He Touched Me   24

7. Divine Intoxication   27

DEDICATION

This book is dedicated with much love and appreciation to some dear friends whose hearts and homes have been opened to me and my family:

THOMAS and CHRISTINE

JOHN and EUNICE

JOHN and ELIZABETH

"It is right for me to feel this way about all of you, since I have you in my heart . . . all of you share in God's grace with me". (Philippians 1:7)

PREFACE

There is a growing interest today in the ongoing ministry of the Holy Spirit. For too long, He has been the forgotten factor in the life of the Church. Yet, allied to this resurgence of curiosity, there is apparently a conscious failure on the part of many to understand what His role is in their daily lives. To counteract this serious deficiency these vital truths are expounded in the chapters that follow.

If, as a result of reading this small volume, your eyes are opened to a greater awareness of His Person and Work, then the author's prayers will have been answered, and, to Him be all the glory and praise.

SAMUEL GORDON
Loughborough, Leicestershire
October 1986

Chapter One
A CHANGE OF ADDRESS

John Owen is said to have expressed the opinion that the sin of Old Testament times was a failure to acknowledge God, the sin of the New Testament era was an unwillingness to recognise the Lordship of Christ, and the obvious sin of his times was man's lack of appreciation of the ministry of the Holy Spirit relative to personal experience. As it was then, so it is now! Times haven't really changed! He, the Holy Spirit, is still the neglected member of the Trinity.

In an attempt to make amends, I want to share with you some relevant insights from the Word of God. That's always the best place to start! It is most instructive to read of Him no fewer than four times described as, *"the seven Spirits of God"* (cf. Revelation 1:4). What does this suggest?

It certainly does not mean there are seven Holy Spirits active in God's dealings with His children. That's out of the question altogether! There is only one but His operations are construed as being sevenfold. This heptagonal manifestation is seen best in the seven terms employed in the Scriptures to set forth His mission in relation to the people of God. We shall look at each of these in succeeding chapters. By the way, the *"seven"* would indicate the perfection of His work and would imply the plenitude of His power.

The first is spelled out clearly in I Corinthians 12:13 and speaks of the Baptism in the Holy Spirit. This is what Paul says: *"For we were all baptised by one Spirit into one body — whether Jews or Greeks, slave or free — and we were all given the one Spirit to drink".* This aspect signifies:

IMMERSION

There are seven main passages in the Word which speak of this wonderful truth. Four are found in the Gospels, two in the Acts of the Apostles, and, one (quoted above) in the Epistles. Each of the Gospel writers distinctly show the words were uttered by John the Baptist, and are used to underline the contrast between what John is doing and what Jesus will do (cf. Matthew 3:11; Mark 1:8; Luke 3:16; John 1:33). However, in Acts 1:5, the reverse is the case when Jesus categorically affirms: *"For John baptised with water, but in a few days you will be baptised with the Holy Spirit".* These all view the issue prophetically. It was something not yet experienced or even bestowed. It was, from their vantage point, a happening that lay ahead. The emphasis is on the words, *"He will . . ."* and, that is future in its outlook.

The single reference in the Epistles represents the doctrinal viewpoint. The tense of the verb is of paramount importance to us in our search for the underlying meaning of what Paul is stating. Let's be clear, he does not say, 'we shall be', or, 'we may be', or, 'we ought to be'. Rather, he says, *"we were"*, and, since this is in the aorist tense it suggests an accomplished fact. As far as this passage is concerned, the Baptism in the Spirit, is connected not with our state as Christians, but with our standing. This is the occasion and means of our incorporation into the mystical Body of Christ. So, Paul conclusively sees this as a finished work. Because it is a completed task it is a once-for-all occurrence!

Most references point forward, one points backward, but, to what? There must be a focal point where they merge together. That's why we turn to the Book of Acts (ch. 2:1—4) where we view this great event from a historical perspective. When Jesus used the words, *"in a few days"*, He was indicating explicitly the Day of Pentecost. Logically speaking, it can't be anything else! On that memorable morn the long-promised Holy Spirit was given and the Church of Christ was brought into being. It was the birthday of the Church. The Body of Christ was formed on that day almost two millennia ago. It was the dawning of a new era, i.e. the age of the Spirit. This is truly a miracle and, in many senses, it is still a mystery to the finite mind. This was the hour when the whole mystical Church was immersed into one body in a never-to-be-repeated experience. You and I enter into the rich blessing and realisation of that ancient inauguration when we are saved by God's amazing grace. For us, it is a change of address!

IDENTIFICATION

At the precise moment of our salvation, we become identified with the Body of Christ, the Church universal. How? By being immersed into the Body! This is, take note, not the luxury of an elite few. Rather, none are excluded and no exceptions are made. It is the common lot of God's children. Hence, Paul's wisdom in stressing the word, *all"*.

It would also suggest our unity in Christ. We are *"all one in Christ Jesus"* (Galatians 3:28). We share a common salvation (cf. Jude 3) and rejoice that we are made to *"participate in the divine nature"* (II Peter 1:4). Background or nationality do not alter the fact that we are members of one Body. Yes, irrespective of colour, class or creed, the ground was level at the foot of the cross, and, in Him there is no difference made.

Our union with Christ is also envisaged. We are like branches in the vine (cf. John 15), like living stones in the building (cf. Ephesians 2). And, furthermore, we are joined to Christ, the living Head. That means we share in everything the Father has given to Him. What a privileged position is ours of being, *"co-heirs with Christ"* (Romans 8:17). We are, to borrow a favourite phrase of the apostle Paul, said to be *"in Christ"*.

INTEGRATION

Since there is one Body we have fellowship with each other. The Body, as you would imagine, is comprised of individual members — none of whom can be done without. All are needed to enable the Body to function normally. It is God who places us in the Body and it is the Holy Spirit who gives us different gifts to exercise. That, whether we like it or not, is His sole prerogative and is not dependent on self-centred man with his insatiable desire to walk centre-stage. When these are operating in a manner pleasing to Him then the Body is achieving His eternal purpose for it. Not everyone has the same gift and no-one has a monopoly on all the gifts. We are where He wants us to be and we have what He desires to impart to us (cf. I Corinthians 12 and 14). We all have a vital part to play in glorifying His Name and advancing His cause on planet earth. Where love is the supreme factor then a spirit of competition or divisiveness will be set to the side (cf. I Corinthians 13). Actually, it will be a case of each for the other and together for God!

This will be manifest in our attitude to each other. We ought to be a caring community sharing and showing concern for our brothers and sisters in the family. A mutual interest in the other person's welfare is what Paul has in view in I Corinthians 12:26, *"If one part suffers, every part suffers with it; if one part is honoured, every part rejoiceth with it".* In the light of Paul's argument we probably need to make an urgent reappraisal of our inter-personal relationships within the context of the Body of Christ.

That's what the Baptism in the Holy Spirit is all about — our being placed into the Body of Christ. What a tremendous privilege! But, oh, what a weighty responsibility is placed upon our shoulders!

Chapter Two
GOD'S LOVE GIFT

Time after time we thank God for the gift of the Son of His love. And rightly so! Surely this is a gift which is indescribable and One which is full of grace and glory. None can be compared to Jesus!

Day by day we likewise lift our hearts in praise and thankfulness to God for the gift of *"such a great salvation"* (Hebrews 2:3). Certainly this is a gift of infinite and eternal value and is a priceless treasure to cherish.

All too often, though, we forget to thank our Heavenly Father for the gift of the Holy Spirit. Here is a gift whose worth cannot be measured. Apart and aside from Him we can do absolutely nothing. The saintly Samuel Chadwick aptly comments, ''The gift of the Holy Spirit is the crowning mercy of God in Christ Jesus. It was for this all the rest was. The incarnation and crucifixion, the resurrection and ascension, were all preparatory to Pentecost. Without the gift of the Holy Spirit all the rest would be useless. The great thing in Christianity is the gift of the Spirit''. And, so say all of us!

Peter makes it abundantly clear in his forthright preaching on the Day of Pentecost that prior to receiving the Holy Spirit there must be repentance on our part (cf. Acts 2:38). We resolve to turn our back on our sin and embrace the free offer of Christ in the Gospel. Only then, and not before it, will the Holy Spirit be given to us. You see, the Son glorifies the Father, the Spirit glorifies the Son, and, only then can Christ by the Holy Spirit be glorified in us. Indeed, Calvary opened the fountain from which poured forth the full blessing of Pentecost.

When we receive Him as a gift we do not receive Him in stages or at different intervals. We receive a Person who comes to abide within us. And, common-sense dictates, no-one can receive a Person by instalments! It is good to remember that He is there to stay causing our hearts to become His permanent residence (cf. John 14:16, 17). He is our Eternal Inhabitant!

It is His responsibility to make Christ real to us (cf. John 16:13—15) so that each day spent in touch with Him will be more meaningful than the day before. He will lead us into deeper depths with the Lord. He will guide our footsteps on to the higher plane where Christ becomes everything to us.

A chapter that never fails to intrigue me is Romans 8. It is from beginning to end full of the Holy Spirit. He is mentioned no fewer than nineteen times! This discourse from the pen of Paul explains to us the way of victory. There we discover the secret to living a life of overcoming. The Holy Spirit is at the hub and all revolves around Him. Look afresh and consider:

HE IS POWERFUL

This monumental chapter is the Christian's declaration of freedom. The inspired writer elaborates on the theme of the liberty we have in Christ and painstakingly shows that we are free from judgement (cf. vs. 1—4). In Adam we were all condemned but in Christ *"there is now no condemnation".* The Law could not save us but the Lord can! In verses 5 to 17 there is freedom from defeat. We are under no obligation to the old nature and so long as we starve it and feed the new nature we can live in triumph on the victory side. Then, he draws our attention to a three-fold groaning (cf. vs. 18—30) and reminds us of a freedom from discouragement. Creation, Christians and the Comforter have this in common but for us a better day is coming! Finally, we are assured that there is a freedom from fear in verses 31 to 39. We are kept by His power. We are secure in the love of Christ from where no-one or nothing can separate us. Where the Spirit we have been given is Lord in our lives then we shall enormously enjoy this vast expanse of liberty (cf. II Corinthians 3:17).

HE IS PRECIOUS

We have been brought into the family of God and how glad we are! We have received *"the spirit of sonship"* (Romans 8:15). In other words, having been adopted, we are like adult sons in His family. It is true that at the moment of our salvation we are *"like newborn babies"* (I Peter 2:2) and the need is imperative that we grow into mature believers, but, at the same time, He sees us as adult children who are able to enjoy all the benefits He has in store for us here and now!

When we are baptised in the Spirit we are placed as members in the Body of Christ. When we receive the gift of the Spirit we are placed as sons in the family of Christ.

Because we belong to the worldwide family of God it means the Holy Spirit will lead us (cf. Romans 8:14). he will guide us in the way we ought to go. In the Old Testament God led Israel through the wilderness en-route to the Promised Land and He will do the same for us.

It also means we experience the warmth of the sunshine of the Father's love (cf. Romans 8:15, 16) and cry unto Him, *"abba"*. This delightful phrase can be translated into our mother tongue to mean 'dada' and carries with it the idea of trust and dependence. That's the kind of intimacy we have with Him. John Gill observes that the word "abba" reads backwards the same as forwards, implying that God is the Father of His people in adversity as well as prosperity. The reason why we respond in such a manner is because *"the Spirit Himself testifies with our spirit that we are God's children"* (Romans 8:16). In Hebrews 10:15 He witnesses TO us and that's based on fact; in I John 5:10 He witnesses IN us and that is based on faith; but, in the verse alluded to already He witnesses WITH us and that is founded on feelings. Is it any wonder we joyfully cry, *"abba"*? Ah, the hymnwriter summed it up well when he wrote:

"My God is reconciled;
His pardoning voice I hear:
He owns me for His child;
I can no longer fear:
With confidence I now draw nigh,
And 'Father, Abba Father!' cry".

13

HE IS PRAYERFUL

Because we have received the gift of the Holy Spirit it means we have One within our hearts who can lay bare before the eyes of the Lord the deepest need of our souls. Most of us at one time or another, if we are honest, feel utterly helpless in the realm of prayer — we don't know how to pray, we don't know when to pray, we don't know where to pray, and, we don't know what to pray. That's one reason why we have the gift of the Holy Spirit so that He can come to our aid.

He is the Comforter, or, the ''Paraclete'', the One called alongside to help and strengthen. His undertaking is shown in our weakness when *"He Himself intercedes for us with groans that words cannot express"* (Romans 8:26). Yes, praise the Lord, He prays for us and He prays within us (cf. Romans 8:27). What a marvellous ministry He lovingly exercises in our lives without creating an atmosphere where we feel uncomfortably inferior.

It was A. T. Pierson who said, ''The Holy Spirit was God's ascension gift to Christ, that He might be bestowed by Christ, as His ascension gift to the Church''. Have you whispered a genuine 'thank you' for Him yet?

Chapter Three
UNDER NEW MANAGEMENT

"Soon as my all I ventured,
On the atoning blood.
The Holy Spirit entered —
And I was born of God."

The sentiments of the above chorus highlight for us another phase of the Holy Spirit's operation in that it speaks of His Indwelling. To put it simply, that suggests: He makes our hearts His home, our bodies become His temple, these mortal frames become the sanctuary of the Living God, our hearts become the very house of God. We can realistically affirm, *"we have this treasure in jars of clay to show that this all-surpassing power is from God and not from us"* (II Corinthians 4:7). Our spirit becomes the permanent nest for God's holy Dove!

The Biblical teaching on this aspect of His sovereign work is seen in the writings of Paul to the Christians in the city of Corinth where he says, *"Don't you know that you yourselves are God's temple and that God's Spirit lives in you"* (I Corinthians 3:16); and, again, *"Do you not know that your body is a temple of the Holy Spirit, who is in you, whom you have received from God"* (I Corinthians 6:19). This duo of references causes us to ponder the fact that:

HE IS THE COMFORTER — HE MINISTERS TO US

This is the thought captured by the hymnwriter in that familiar stanza:

"Our blest Redeemer, ere He breathed,
His tender last farewell;
A Guide, a Comforter bequeathed,
With us to dwell."

But, there is more to it than that! Not only is He with us, according to John 14:17, He *"will be in us".* Every believer, no matter who they are or what they are, has Him residing within as the Comforter. It is interesting to note that in John 14:26 He is the gift of the Father, whilst, in John 15:26 He is said to be the gift of the Son. He is sometimes seen as the Spirit of God, the Spirit of Christ, or, the Spirit of His Son. Whatever the title adopted, the peculiar ministry in which He is engaged is clear for all to see. Yes, He ministers Christ to us! That means:

When we are lonely, He gives us a sense of the presence of Christ;
When we are worried, He turns our thoughts to the Person of Christ;
When we are afraid, He shares with us the peace of Christ;
When we are weak, He helps us draw from the power of Christ;
When we are downcast, He tells us about the prayers of Christ;
When we are uncertain, He causes us to reflect on the purpose of Christ;
When we are doubting, He assures us of the provision of Christ;
When we are tossed about, He steadies us with the promises of Christ.

HE IS THE CONFORMER — HE MOULDS US

This is undeniably one of the great eternal purposes of God for each of His children. He desires that we would become increasingly more and more like Jesus. That's why we have been predestinated, so that *"we might be conformed to the likeness of His Son"* (Romans 8:29). He longs that we might project to others something of the image of Christ. Paul's crowning ambition for the saints at Galatia was to see Christ formed in them (cf. Galatians 4:19).

This must be the major incentive of every Christian, young or old. To show forth the loveliness of His dear Son should be our main objective in this life. To reflect to a greater degree the intrinsic beauties of Jesus ought to be the occupation to which we tirelessly devote our energy.

How does He do it? That's always the six million dollar question! He purifies us in the fiery furnace of affliction so that we are more refined afterward than we were before. He moulds us in the crucible of daily experience causing us to realise *"that in all things God works for the good of those who love Him"* (Romans 8:28). He fashions us with all the care and skill of a Potter so that He might produce *"an instrument (or, vessel) for noble purposes useful to the Master"* (II Timothy 2:21).

HE IS THE CONTROLLER — HE MASTERS US

The salutary lesson we learn from this aspect of His work in us is that, we *"are not our own"*. Why? We *"were bought with a price"* (I Corinthians 6:19, 20). What is the purchase price? *"The precious blood of Christ"* (I Peter 1:19). Yes, we belong to Him! We are His property and possesion. We are, believe it or not, owned by Him!

Therefore, if God is to be glorified in us, it means we can't live the way we like, we dare not do what we want, we must not go our own way. It's a hard and difficult lesson to grasp as experience reminds all of us! We should be under His absolute sway and under His authority and control. It is all for Christ because in the Spirit we have all of Christ!

Sin should no longer have dominion over us; Satan should no more have his say in our hearts: the world should not demand our attention and appeal to us; and, the flesh should not gain the upper hand . . . with Him inside us, we are under new management!

HE IS THE CHALLENGER — HE MOTIVATES US

Paul throws down the gauntlet by issuing a strong challenge to each of us to live lives that will win His smile of approval. The Lord's return is nearer as the minutes tick by. Therefore, we must be aware of the solemn possibility that we could defile the temple which is sacred to Him (cf. I Corinthians 3:17).

When we fall foul of His perfect plan for our lives we limit His power at work in us thereby grieving and hurting the Holy Spirit. Significantly, we also quench His Spirit, as we extinguish the fire of God in our souls and we become like damp squibs!

Defilement carries with it the idea of impurity or uncleanness and implies the vessel is dirty. When we think wrong thoughts, dabble in our favourite sin, allow old habits to remain unbroken, we are well on our way to becoming tainted with the dust of the devil. A church building is the house of God — so, too are our bodies; therefore, what is good for one is appropriate for the other! He lives in us! Oh, as others would fix their gaze on us, may they see an unspoilt portrait of Jesus.

Chapter Four
HEAVEN'S ROYAL CREST

The title may seem rather strange to the uninitiated. But it conveys a truth Paul mentioned in his letter to the saints at Ephesus when he said, *"Having believed, you were marked in Him, with a seal, the promised Holy Spirit"* (Ephesians 1:13; cf. 4:30). This fourth aspect of His work is, like the previous three, instantaneous with the moment of our salvation and signifies from that time onward we bear His crest upon our souls. Consequently, it carries with it the idea of security.

Permit me to digress a little and share a couple of other instances recorded on the pages of Scripture that deserve our consideration. There is:

THE SON'S SEAL

In John 6:27 we read, *"On Him God the Father has placed His seal of approval".* Three times at least during his brief ministry on earth did the Father assure the son of His love and care for Him. There was the occasion of His baptism in the River Jordan, then, later on the Mount of Transfiguration, and, finally, a few steps before He began the ascent of Calvary when His soul was troubled, did the heavens open. Literally, out of the blue, a voice was heard to say: *"This is My Son, whom I love; with Him I am well pleased"* (cf. Matthew 3:16, 17; Luke 9:35; John 12:27, 28).

The Father was publicly stamping His seal of approval on the redeeming work of His only Son. Surely this was a seal of confirmation and shows to us the mark of the Father's inherent pleasure in the life of His Son.

THE SERVANT'S SEAL

In Revelation 7:2 the exiled John on the Isle of Patmos describes a scene where a vast company of people bear the seal of God upon their foreheads. This divine imprimatur was a mark of identification. You see, God never leaves Himself without a witness. Even in the darkest hour of this world's history there is raised up a godly remnant from within the nation of Israel. There are one hundred and forty-four thousand who will unashamedly show their allegiance to the Lord Jesus. Twelve thousand from each of the twelve tribes are branded with the insignia of the King of Kings and Lord of Lords. These endtime Jewish missionaries will complete the task of world evangelisation before the King returns in power and glory. These are authentic witnesses of Jehovah to the far flung corners of the earth.

In these two separate illustrations we have the seal used to indicate the Father's delight in the achievement of His Son and, latterly, the Father's intention to identify a certain company as belonging to Him. Now, let's go back to where we started and grasp another strand of precious truth.

THE SAINTS SEAL

The double reference in the epistle to the Ephesians has already been underscored but there is another. The same apostle goes a step further when writing to Timothy, his son in the faith, by teaching that, *"God's solid foundation stands firm, sealed with this inscription: 'The Lord knows those who are His' "* (II Timothy 2:19). How apt are the words of the hymn:

"Then on each He setteth,
His own secret sign,
They who have My Spirit,
These, saith He, are mine."

Therefore, the Holy Spirit of God, is the Seal of our salvation. This suggests four things:

FAITH'S REASON

We are saved because of Calvary. We are born again because of love's redemptive work on Golgotha's brow. We are made right with God because of what was accomplished on that centre Cross. It was there a work was finished. There remaineth no more to be done for Jesus paid it all! It speaks of a completed transaction. We are where we are, we are what we are, we are whose we are, by the grace of God.

FAITH'S RICHNESS

Since we are resting on the solid rock of a finished work, all is well with our souls. Not only are we baptised in the Spirit, not only have we been made the recipients of the gift of the Spirit, not only are we indwelt by the Spirit — but, to crown it all, the Father sets His seal upon our salvation. That seal is the Person of the divine Spirit.

It shows we belong to God. We are His purchased possession. We are owned by Him and the Father is consciously aware of His children's identity. With some folks we wonder about the genuineness of their conversion; with others we question the sincerity of their profession of faith; with a few we doubt the reality of their experience of saving grace. So much seems to be so hollow and superficial that it just doesn't ring true. But, this truth teaches us, that God knows!

FAITH'S REALITY

The genuine article always bears the seal. That seal cannot be broken. That seal cannot be severed. And so, it naturally follows, since we have been washed in the blood of the Lamb and brought into God's wonderful family — and, sealed, that we are eternally secure in the Lord Jesus. Our life in Him is everlasting. His life in us is eternal. And, eternity is never ending. That means, we will always belong to Him.

FAITH'S REWARD

It's good to remind ourselves often that we are *"sealed for the day of redemption"* (Ephesians 4:30). A better day is coming when faith will give way to sight, when symbols will disappear to be replaced by glorious reality. There is for the Lord's elect the prospect of Glory at the end of the road.

Yes, praise God, our life is secure because the Spirit is the seal of our salvation. How wonderful to know that we have the royal crest of Heaven upon our hearts.

> "All glory be to Jesus' name,
> I know that He is mine;
> For on my heart the Spirit seals,
> His pledge of love Divine."

Chapter Five
ENGAGED TO BE MARRIED

The fifth word employed in the canon of Scripture to speak of the Spirit's work in relation to God's people is that of the *"deposit"*. He is quaintly described in some earlier translations as the *"earnest"*. We read about this in such passages as Ephesians 1:14; II Corinthians 1:22; 5:5. It is a term pregnant with meaning.

In the previous chapter we noted that the *"seal"* assures us we belong to Christ. The *"deposit"* reminds us Christ belongs to us! Listen to the romantic language of the Song of Solomon 2:16, *"My lover is mine and I am His"*. The same concept is voiced by the hymnwriter:

> "Dear Saviour, Thou art mine,
> How sweet the thought to me."

Paul writing in Romans 8:23 says we have *"the first fruits of the Spirit"*. Acting in this capacity, He is a foretaste of all the Lord has in store for His own. He is virtually promising us days of Heaven upon earth. The luscious grapes the spies brought back from Canaan were an indication of what awaited them in the land of promise. So, the Holy Spirit, as the *"Deposit"* is the foretaste of heavenly fulness. He gives us a sample of all that is to follow in Immanuel's Land.

> "Blessed assurance, Jesus is mine,
> Oh what a foretaste of glory divine."

He is also likened to an engagement ring (hence the chapter heading). This suggests a covenant between two parties in an agreement which is binding. There is no broken engagement as far as He is concerned! The promise of the forthcoming marriage will be honoured. There will be no last minute postponement or hitches. Christ is the Groom, the Church is His bride, and, in that day, He will come and claim her for Himself. Then will take place the wedding of all the ages! As we await that day, we are said to be engaged to Christ. What a loving relationship that is! While we are absent from Him our love grows stronger and deeper as we anticipate the joyful moment of fulfilment.

But, that's not all! He is, as I have hinted already, likened to a deposit that has been paid or a guarantee that has been given. He is, in one sense, the first instalment. Still there's more to follow! What God has already given in part, He will bestow at last in perfection. Now we have the initial experience, but the present enjoyment of Him is a pledge of future bliss. This means He has given us the assurance that *"He will fulfil His purpose for us"* (cf. Psalm 138:8) and eventually, in His time, bring us into the Father's home. We can say with Paul, *"Being confident of this, that He who began a good work in you will carry it on to completion until the day of Christ Jesus"* (Philippians 1:6).

Yes, there is some delay before the final goods are delivered — but, if the sample is anything to go by, the rest is worth waiting for! The inheritance is ours now but we don't enter into it until then. We have the thrilling prospect of a better life awaiting us when we cross over the sea of death to the mainland of Heaven. Now, we have grace . . . then, it will be glory! But, after all, grace is glory begun in the soul!

As we think about this we are convinced that "the Lord is able to give us much more than this". The words of the chorus are a fine example of what we have been meditating upon:

"If here it is so blessed —
What will it be up there"?

In the deposit of the Holy Spirit we have a little piece of Heaven to go to Heaven with. Charles H. Spurgeon fittingly commented, "Little faith will take our souls to Heaven, but great faith will bring Heaven to our souls". That's the primary function of Him as a "deposit".

We are born for Glory. We are bound for Glory. And, what a moment, when we shall see Him for the very first time! I often reflect on the words of the hymn and how appropriate they are in this setting:

"Once Heaven seemed a far off place,
Till Jesus showed His smiling face.
Now it's begun within my soul —
'Twill last while endless ages roll''.

Over there is the wonder of:

HIS PERSON

Heaven will afford us the unspeakable opportunity of eternally beholding the King in all His unparalleled beauty. There communion will be unbroken. There fellowship will be uninhibited and unlimited. There we shall enjoy for ever and ever Him in all the glory of Who He really is. We shall be taken up with the Lamb. Now, our eyes are dimmed, but, then, face to face!

HIS PRESENCE

Heaven is Heaven because Jesus is there. Never again will He leave the splendour of Heaven. He has gone home, and, when we arrive, we're all there to stay! Then, time will be no more, our troubles and trials will be over, our tears will have dried and we shall be satisfied just to be at His side. Now, in our moments of doubt and fear, in those dark dismal days when the north wind of adversity is blowing, in those lonely hours when everything seems to have fallen apart, He comes very close to us! That's just a fleeting glimpse of what it will be like in a day to come.

HIS PRECIOUSNESS

It is so difficult to imagine and so hard to visualise in the mind's eye what it will be like when we step out on the golden strand of Heaven. We shall extol His virtues, we shall exalt His victories, and, overwhelmed, we shall fall down and worship him for He is Lord of all. Now, *"to we who believe, this stone is precious"* (I Peter 2:7). Why is that? Because as the Deposit He has given to us a foretaste and an inkling of that which lies before us. He becomes sweeter as the days go by. The joy He gives is unspeakable and inexpressible, the peace He bestows transcends all understanding, the love He shares surpasses knowledge, but, wait for it . . . the best is yet to be!

Ah, my friend, Christ belongs to us. Heaven has been born in our souls and each step we take is one step nearer the final destination. He actually makes us homesick for Heaven!

> "Mine, mine, mine,
> I know Thou art mine,
> Saviour, dear Saviour,
> I know Thou art mine".

Chapter Six
HE TOUCHED ME

The title I have selected is well known to all and sundry as being the name of one of Bill and Gloria Gaither's musical compositions. But, perhaps, the truth is not so familiar. I refer to the Anointing of the Holy Spirit.

These are days of unprecedented opportunity for the Lord's people. The return of the Lord, many believe, is imminent. He is building His Church. We need to be alert and face up to the challenge of the lateness of the hour. In fact, it has never been so late before! We need to move out and win men and women for Jesus. The pressing need is for Christians anointed with the Holy Spirit to go out into the highways and byways laying the sinner low and lifting the Saviour high.

It is instructive to note that there is a subtle difference bewveen the anointing and the fulness of the Holy Spirit. The anointing is something extra! It is an added bonus! It is more than a filling. This truth is clarified when we view the encounters of our blessed Lord with the Holy Spirit. He was filled with the Holy Spirit from birth, but it was only when He started His public ministry thirty years later that He was anointed on the banks of the Jordan river.

If you like, the anointing is outward and the filling is inward. The former is upon Christ, whilst, the latter is in Christ. An illustration of this is seen in Leviticus 2 where the Meal Offering is dealt with. It, typically, speaks of the loveliness of the life of Christ. We read of the *"fine flour mingled with oil"* and that symbolises the fulness of the Holy Spirit. Likewise, we read they were to *"pour oil upon it"* and that is highly suggestive of the Spirit's anointing ministry. The oil is often used in the Old Testament as a representation of the Holy Spirit of God.

When Peter made his epic confession and declared unequivocally with no strings attached. *"Thou art the Christ"*, he was saying to Jesus: *"Thou art the Anointed One"* (cf. Matthew 16:16). Under the old economy the Old Testament prophets were anointed to be the messengers of God to the people, the priests were anointed to serve and to be enabled to live lives of holiness before the Lord, and, the kings were anointed so that the Holy Spirit might rest upon them in power. Compare this trio of ideas with the Lord Jesus Christ. As Prophet, He was anointed that He might bring to us the living Word of God; as Priest, He was anointed that He might represent us in the immediate presence of God; as King, He was anointed that He might rule and reign in our hearts.

Matthew 12:18 lets us go behind the scenes. There we read of Him: *"Here is My Servant whom I have chosen"* — yes, He is the appointed One; *"The One I love, in whom I delight"* — yes, He is the approved One; and, *"I will put My Spirit on Him . . ."* — yes, He is the anointed One!

Come with me for a moment to the local synagogue in Nazareth. On a certain sabbath Jesus was called to read the lesson based on Isaiah 61:1, 2. When He finished He closed the book and sat down. The response was breathtaking. It says, *"The eyes of everyone were fastened on Him . . . all spoke well of Him and were amazed at the gracious words that came from His lips"* (Luke 4:20, 22). Is it any wonder, because standing before them moments earlier was the fulfilment of this wonderful old prophecy. The Book had come alive! What did it mean for Him?

HIS PROCLAMATION

He had a message to preach. He always had something to say. Under the anointing of the Spirit He ministered to all who came across His pathway. Here was God speaking to man through His Son! What was the substance and content of His expositions? It was a fourfold message covering: the gospel of God . . . *"good news"*. He never hesitated to point men to Calvary. This was the best news their ears could ever hear. He spoke of the gift of God . . . *"to proclaim freedom"*. Salvation speaks of freedom and deliverance from bondage to self, sin and Satan. Liberty for those held captive was what He offered to those in His audience. He also stresses the grace of God . . . *"the year of the Lord's favour"*. This was a reference to the moment when God stepped into time at the Incarnation. He was definitely doing man a great favour! He also addressed in the course of His ministry the solemn matter of the gloom of God . . . *"a day of vengeance"*. He often reminded men of a coming time of judgement if they failed to acknowledge Him as Lord in their lives. His message is all-embracing and contains in miniature the embryo of the Gospel of God according to Romans chapter one.

HIS POWER

All Heaven was at His disposal. The mighty reservoir of God's greatness was waiting to be tapped. All the resources of the Creator and Sustainer of the universe are freely available to Him. He could do anything! He can do anything! He came to set men free, to loose the chains that bound them, to break the shackles that gripped them, to snap the fetters that kept them in bondage. His was a daring rescue operation to pluck men out — to lift men up — and, to set their feet on the Rock of Ages.

HIS PITY

He was on more than one occasion moved with deep compassion as He saw the crowds aimlessly wandering like *"sheep without a shepherd"*. The tears often ran down His ruddy cheeks leaving a stained complexion when His heart was stirred and touched. There were times when He broke down and sobbed when He beheld the devastating effect of sin on men and women.

His was a ministry of *"binding up"*, of pouring in the oil to encourage and cheer, as He delicately sought to mend broken hearts. To the bereaved gripped with a sense of plight and sorrow He had a special word and showed a real interest in their predicament. Some were cast down and passing through bouts of dark depression with no seeming light at the end of the tunnel and to them He gave a *"a garment of praise"*. Thank God, in every situation, He is the great Undertaker!

In the light of all that is happening around us in this closing quarter of the twentieth century, do we have His touch upon our lives? If the Prince of preachers needed the unction of the Holy Spirit of God, how much more do we need a similar enduement of power from on high?

"O Holy Spirit, come,
Anoint us one and all,
And let some mighty deed be done,
While at Thy feet we fall."

Chapter Seven
DIVINE INTOXICATION

This chapter brings our studies to a close. In a sense this is a fitting climax to our meditations as it brings each of us to a place of yieldedness before the risen Lord. The Spirit-filled life is the normal Christian experience and is one that brings in its wake the unsurpassed blessing of a surrendered life. When we are abandoned to Him then we permit Him to monopolise and master us. We sometimes sing the hymn which is really a prayer:

"Jesus, fill now with Thy Spirit,
Hearts that full surrender know".

What does it mean to be filled with the Holy Spirit? Again, we go back to the Word of God to find the answer to such a pertinent question. When we turn to Ephesians chapter five we are confronted with a most interesting situation. This great experience of the Spirit's fulness is set in a most remarkable context. It is not just something to be preached from the pulpit, but, is essential for everyday living among men.

With reference to husbands and wives and parents and children He leads to happiness in our hearts and holiness in our homes. When management and employees are talked of, Paul sees the Spirit's fulness leading to the ideal situation of healthy relationships in business life.

This is the life that wins! This is the abundant life in Jesus. This is the life of walking with God, of lingering near the Cross, of staying close to the Saviour's side. This is living in the place where God answers prayer and where we are in constant touch with the almightiness of God (cf. Psalm 91:1).

THE COMMAND

In fact in Ephesians 5:18 there are two commands given. One is negative and the other is positive. *"Do not get drunk on wine, which leads to debauchery. Instead, be filled with the Spirit".* Nothing could be plainer or more pointed than that! In other words, don't get drunk with the Devil's booze, don't even allow his liquor to pass between your lips. BUT, get intoxicated with the new wine of the Spirit of God. Let the cup of your life be full and running over!

This is not something optional. It is obligatory! It is a must for every child of God. Not one individual is an exception to the rule God lays down. From the youngest to the oldest this is an order to be obeyed.

The tense of the verb is fascinating. It is in the present continuous and Paul is saying, "Go on being filled". It is not an initial and final happening. It is a day-by-day, moment-by-moment filling of the Holy Spirit. It is not a once-for-all experience but is something continual and to be continued!

The *"baptism"* was an immersion in the Spirit and emphasised our relationship to Him. The *"anointing"* is an investment of the Spirit and is geared towards our responsibility in service for Christ. The *"fulness"* is an infilling of the Spirit and enables and equips us to enter into a realisation of all that we are and have in Him. Having been apprehended we need to appropriate!

It was as they were filled with the Holy Spirit that all that the Lord was in the value of His Cross, in the victory of His resurrection, in the virtue of His ascension, became real in them. That's why in Acts 2 their joy knew no bounds as they spoke with loosed tongues of *"the wonders of God"* (cf. Acts 2:1—13).

Perhaps the greatest sin of the unbeliever is his refusal to accept new life in Christ. The greatest sin of the believer may be his refusal of life super abounding in the Holy Spirit's fulness.

THE CONTRAST

Three times over the perils of the devil's drink are contrasted with the inestimable pleasures to be found when we drink deeply from the well of His salvation. What is there about a drunkard that Paul sees as important? He loses self-consciousness. When the believer is filled with the Spirit he is lost in Jesus and Christ becomes everything to him. The drunkard loses self-control. The Christian is led by Him and God, by the Spirit, is the Master of his life. The drunkard loses self-conceit. There is no place for pride or presumption or a false humility in the character of the spiritual believer. The Christian ought to be someone who is captivated by Christ, motivated for Christ, and activated by the Spirit of Christ.

The life in the Spirit's fulness is not one of dejection, despair, or even defeat. There are no 'mornings after the night before'. Hangovers are conspicuous by their absence when Christ is Governor of our lives.

THE CONDITIONS

Before we can know this blessed experience we must observe what Paul brings to our attention. It will mean an emptying on our part. There must be a removal of self and sin before He can fill us. ''Emptied that Thou should'st fill me'' is how the hymnwriter expressed it. It implies a cleansing (cf. II Timothy 2:21). The vessel unto honour which is acceptable to Him is one that is purged and purified. To be exclusively His would indicate a willingness on our part to give to Him unreservedly every fibre of our being. He wants not limited access but a through road into our lives. Nothing between Him and us is what is envisaged. We need to let the Divine Spirit pervade our being as water fills a sponge. We should allow Him to saturate every part of our lives, expelling everything alien to His will. The Spirit ever fills by displacement! If the conditions are not met in full, then we will not know the reality of the Spirit filling us. We can't expect God to do His part if we fail to keep our part of the bargain! So, we have been warned!

THE CONSEQUENCES

When an individual is filled with the Holy Spirit the change is obvious for those with eyes to see. Look at the incredible difference before and after Pentecost with regard to the disciples of our Lord. Men are filled for the glory of God. Men are filled so that Christ would be exalted. Men are filled so that the Word would be magnified and His name honoured.

Peter was filled so that he might preach for God (cf. Acts 4:8). The first deacons in the early Church were filled so that they might serve God (cf. Acts 6:3). Stephen was filled so that he might suffer and ultimately die as a martyr for God (cf. Acts 7:55). Barnabas was filled so that he might live up to his name and encourage for God (cf. Acts 11:24). Paul was filled so that he might repudiate falsehood for God who is Truth (cf. Acts 13:9). The Christians who turned the world upside down were filled so that they might be helped to live for God (cf. Acts 13:52).

This is, as you will see, the victorious Christian life. When the fulness is overflowing in our lives then sin, self and Satan are conquered foes. We have an overwhelming sense of our personal unworthiness, but, allied to that is the thrill of His preciousness to us. We will be joyful (cf. Ephesians 5:19), thankful (cf. v. 20), and submissive (cf. v. 21) in our hearts, in our homes, and, in the house of God.

Let me ask you, as I ask myself, are we filled with the Holy Spirit? If the answer is "no", why don't you get down on your knees and pray:

> "Have Thine own way, Lord,
> Have Thine own way,
> Hold o'er my being absolute sway.
> Fill with Thy Spirit, till all shall see,
> Christ only, always, living in me".